Miniature
Needlepoint
■ Carpets ■

Miniature
Needlepoint
▪ Carpets ▪

Janet Granger

Guild of Master Craftsman Publications

First published 1996 by
Guild of Master Craftsman Publications Ltd,
166 High Street, Lewes,
East Sussex BN7 1XU

© Janet Granger 1996

ISBN 1 86108 023 9

Photography by Chris Greenwood

Line drawings by John Yates

Designed by Teresa Dearlove

Typeface: Novarese

Origination in Singapore under the supervision of MRM Graphics
Printed and bound by Emirates Printing Press, Dubai

DEDICATION

To my lovely husband, Chris:
thank you for being my best friend
and computer 'guru'.

ACKNOWLEDGEMENTS

I would like to offer my thanks to the following people:
to Peter and Pat Drew of Maple Miniatures, Thaxted, Essex,
for the loan of their own dolls' house, plus others from their
shop (used for some of the room-setting photographs);
to Colin Fulford of Fulford Software Solutions,
for telephone support on his 'Easy Cross'
computer cross stitch design program;
to Liz Inman and Bryony Benier of GMC Publications,
for editorial support, encouragement and good ideas;
to Chris Greenwood, for the photography.

Contents

General Designs

Functional Carpets

Modern Designs

Traditional Designs

Introduction

Your dolls' house is special. Even though you may have admired and longed for dozens of other houses at museums, shows and fairs, your own house is unique to you. It is a way of expressing your ideas, tastes and interests in an unusual and creative setting. Whether you are a stickler for historical detail, or someone who throws together a whole house in a few weeks, everything you choose to put in your dolls' house is your decision, and is therefore a way of saying something about yourself.

Miniaturists have been known to travel hundreds of miles in search of just the right item to complete a room. To outsiders this seems absurd, especially when the price is mentioned. 'How much? But you could get a real one for that!' they cry. Sometimes, of course, although we like to think that money is no object when it comes to our obsession, it really does rule out some of the more coveted items. This certainly tends to be the case with miniature needlework. The materials are not expensive, but the amount of time involved puts much of the exquisite work on the market beyond the reach of many of us. But miniaturists are an inventive lot – if you can't buy it, make it yourself! That is basically how this book came about. I had seen lovely examples of needlepoint carpets at dolls' house fairs, but as I could not afford even the smallest, I decided to have a go myself.

This book contains 25 designs of various styles. They range in complexity from small, simple designs which can be finished in a few evenings and are suitable for complete beginners, to large, challenging designs suitable for those with some needlework experience. Each design has been given a 'difficulty rating' as follows:

★　　A simple design, suitable for beginners
★★　　Some previous needlepoint experience needed
★★★　For experienced stitchers

If you have never attempted needlepoint before, there are intro-ductory sections which cover basic materials and techniques. How to follow the charts is explained on pages 13–14.

Apart from saving money by doing the work yourself, there is a lot of satisfaction to be had from creating something beautiful that will last for years. Also you will have the opportunity to play around with colour schemes, sizing and style, so that your carpet will be custom-made for your own dolls' house. To help with this, I have included a special section on designing your own carpets and using colour (*see* pages 21–26).

Essential Equipment

The list of essential items is not long, but it is worth buying the best you can afford, as economizing on basic materials tends to show in your finished work. It may be tempting to rush to the nearest embroidery shop and buy the lot, but it is better to shop around a bit until you are completely satisfied.

WOOLS AND THREADS

There are many types of wool and thread on the market. I chose to use Appleton's crewel wool for all the carpets shown in this book. It is a fine, two-ply wool and is available from many suppliers in a wide range of colours.

You might choose to work the designs in an alternative thread such as stranded cotton (DMC, for example, is a popular range). This is a mercerized cotton, which means it has a polished sheen. Stranded cotton is made up from six strands twisted together, which can be separated and re-combined to make different thicknesses of thread, or to mix shades. On 18 count canvas (see below) you would need to use between four and six strands in the needle to achieve adequate coverage, or you could decide to use fewer strands to obtain a deliberately threadbare look.

Whatever type of thread or wool you decide to use, always buy enough to complete your project, as batch colours can vary slightly.

CANVAS

All the designs in this book were worked on 18 count interlock canvas. This means that the canvas is woven with 18 threads to the inch (2.5cm) in each direction. Although the canvas is now sold in metres, it is still always described as '18 count', '18 hpi', or 'no.18'. This is the smallest count with which I can work comfortably. It is slightly over scale for exact 1/12 work, but I feel it is a good compromise between accuracy and ruining your eyesight. Even so, using 18 count canvas means there are 324 stitches per square inch (50 stitches per square centimetre)!

To get nearer to an exact 1/12 scale, you may prefer to use 22 count canvas. This will give you a finer carpet, proportionately smaller than one made on 18 count, but as the same two-ply wool is used for both counts, it gets harder to pull the wool through the smaller holes of the finer canvas and the wool wears out more quickly.

To calculate exactly the finished size of any design, you need to know the maximum dimensions in stitches (all the designs in this book give these dimensions). If you divide these measurements by the count of canvas you will be using, the figure you get will be the actual size of the carpet.

Take, for example, a carpet of 132 x 89 stitches. To calculate its size in inches using 22 count canvas, divide 132 by 22 to get 6, and 89 by 22 to get 4.04: your carpet will be about 6 x 4in. To calculate the size of the same carpet done on 18 count canvas, divide 132 by 18 to get 7.33, and 89 by 18 to get 4.94: your carpet will come out at about 7¼ x 5in.

To calculate the size in centimetres, work out the formula above as for imperial measurements, then multiply the final answer by 2.54. For instance, the 18 count carpet in the example above came out at 7¼ x 5in. Multiply each of these figures by 2.54 to get measurements of 18.4 x 12.7cm.

SCISSORS

You will need to have two pairs of scissors: sharp dressmaking scissors for cutting the canvas, and small, pointed embroidery scissors which should be kept solely for cutting threads. It is a good idea to tie a length of ribbon to one of the handles of the embroidery scissors and keep them round your neck, as small scissors have a habit of slipping down the side of the chair just when you need them.

NEEDLES

For needlepoint you should use tapestry needles. These have a large eye and a blunt tip. A size 24 is the correct one to use on 18 count canvas; use a size 26 if working on 22 count. As a rough guide, the threaded needle should be able to pass through the holes of the canvas with only a very slight pressure, but should not be able to slip through on its own. If you are working on one of the designs which has many small areas of colour, it is well worth threading each colour onto a separate needle to avoid the need to keep re-threading one needle.

Needles do get dirty with constant handling, so it is best not to use the same one for ever. For the same reason, try not to store your work with the needle left in the canvas as it could leave a mark. Needles can be cleaned by using a specially made pincushion filled with an abrasive such as emery powder. Poking the needle in and out of this several times should clean away any discoloration.

FRAMES

If you do not usually use a frame, I strongly advise you to start now! There is nothing so demoralizing as spending hours on a piece of embroidery, with most of it scrunched up in one hand as you work on the exposed corner, only to flatten out the canvas and find that what you have made is a bumpy, misshapen failure. Using a frame need not make embroidery an uncomfortable, unwieldy experience. They are not expensive, and if you shop around and get the right sort of frame for you, you will be amazed at the improvement in your work.

The sort of frame you need is a rectangular rotating frame (*see* Fig 1). The one I use is hand-held and has 24in (61cm) rollers and 12in (30.5cm) side bars. There are versions on the market that clamp onto table tops, while others are floor-standing. Try a few out in the shop until you feel comfortable with one. A frame will keep the canvas taut, so that it is easier to keep your stitch tension even. This will prevent the canvas from distorting. Even the largest carpet will be distortion-free when finished if you work it on a frame.

To attach your canvas to the frame as shown in Fig 1, first bind all four edges with masking tape. This will prevent your thread from catching on the rough edges and will stop the canvas from

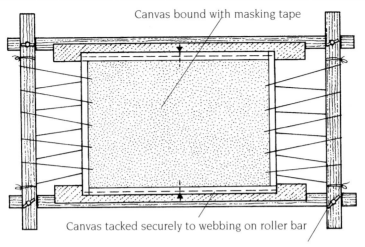

Canvas bound with masking tape

Canvas tacked securely to webbing on roller bar

Fig 1 Fixing the canvas to the rotating frame.

Wing nut to tighten roller bar

fraying. Mark the centre top of the canvas with a light pencil mark and follow a thread line down to the bottom to mark the centre there too. Also mark the centre of the webbing that is fixed to each of the roller bars. Pin the top edge of the canvas to one of the strips of webbing, matching the centre marks, then tack it on securely using strong button thread. Do the same with the bottom edge. Roll each of the bars outwards in turn and tighten the wing nuts to hold them in place. Then lace the canvas to the side bars, making stitches through the canvas about 1in (2.5cm) apart. Tie off securely. If you have tightened the bars enough, the canvas should just about 'bounce' when flicked with a finger. You may find that for very small projects the side lacing is unnecessary.

In the instructions for each carpet, the size of canvas needed is given. This is the minimum, and only allows a 2in (5cm) margin along each side. If you are going to use a frame, you will need to work out how much extra canvas to cut so that it will reach the roller bars on your particular size of frame. For instance, if a carpet measures 5in (12.5cm) wide by 7in (18cm) long, the

amount of canvas needed will be stated as 9in (23cm) wide by
11in (28cm). But if you want to work this on a frame that has bars
12in (30.5cm) apart, you must allow a total length of at least 13in
(33cm) to be able to attach it properly. Obviously, if your frame
has bars narrower than the design, you can wind the extra canvas
around the roller bars and expose one section at a time.

STITCH RIPPER

A stitch ripper is a useful piece of equipment for those
depressing times when you realize you have skipped a stitch in
your pattern, and have been gaily completing row after row of
stitches, all one stitch to the left of where they should have been.
A stitch ripper is better than using embroidery scissors to unpick
with, as it has a very sharp, curved blade on the upper edge. You
can isolate one stitch with it and cleanly slice it from beneath,
without the risk of cutting into the canvas as well.

FABRIC GLUE

I feel that a clear fabric glue such as Fray Check is an essential
item to have. You should find various makes easily obtainable
from needlework suppliers. Fabric glue is a colourless liquid
which prevents unravelling when applied to cut canvas edges. It
has the advantage over conventional glues that it is totally
invisible once dry and will withstand washing. For carpets of an
unusual shape, which cannot be hemmed in the usual way, it is
invaluable (*see* pages 17–18).

OTHER EQUIPMENT

It is a well-known fact that once you have become absorbed in a
hobby, collecting all the equipment is part of the fun. There are
many gadgets available for embroiderers, some far more effective
than others.

There are various kinds of thread storage systems: some people use ring binders and plastic pockets; some use boxes with bobbins, onto which the thread is wound. Particularly if you become interested in designing your own work, you will want to have your threads in an organized form so that you can identify shades quickly and easily.

Also for those who want to design, shade cards are a great source of inspiration for unusual colour combinations.

Daylight simulation bulbs are a good investment. They can be fixed like a normal light bulb into an existing socket, and give a much less yellow light than ordinary artificial lighting. This makes it much easier to see pale colours especially, so that you can keep stitching well into the small hours!

Basic Techniques

PREPARING THE CANVAS

Having decided what count of canvas to use, cut carefully along a thread line using dressmaking scissors, to give a piece large enough to take the design, plus 2in (5cm) on each side. Do not skimp on this fabric allowance, as you will need the extra if you find that you need to block the finished work (*see* pages 15–16). As I mentioned earlier in the section on frames, the edges of the canvas need to be bound with masking tape before you begin to stitch, to prevent fraying. This applies whether you intend to use a frame or not. Almost all the designs are worked from the centre outwards. To find the centre of the canvas, fold it in half both ways, creasing it lightly as you go. The centre is where the two lines cross.

PREPARING THE THREADS

Whether you intend to use wool or stranded cotton, I would suggest that you keep each thread length to between 12in (30cm) and 15in (38cm). The constant pulling of the thread through the canvas quickly weakens it and anything longer than this is likely to break.

To thread your needle, hold it in one hand and loop the thread around the top of the needle, pulling it taut and holding it flat between the thumb and first finger of the other hand. Pull the needle downwards out of the loop, and push the loop through the eye of the needle. Never put thread ends in your mouth to dampen them – it is a very bad habit!

To keep your carpet as flat and neat as possible, do not use knots at the back of the work to secure the thread when starting a new length. Instead, knot the thread but take the needle from the front to the back, about half an inch (1.5cm) away from where you intend to start stitching, then work towards the knot, securing the underlying thread as you go. When you reach the knot you can simply snip it off.

Try not to stitch right to the very end of available thread each time. The last four inches (10cm) or so will be worn by then, and should not be used. Finish off by running the needle through a few stitches on the back of the work.

Try to keep your stitch tension even by working in good light, in a relaxed position.

TYPES OF STITCH USED

There are only two stitches to master, each having their own particular uses, and when completed they both look the same from the front. The difference lies in the direction of the threads on the back of the work, and the effect this has on the tension.

TENT STITCH

Tent stitch is best for the detailed areas. It leaves a long, diagonal pattern of threads on the back. Worked in horizontal and vertical rows, it does tend to distort the canvas a little if you do not use a frame. Fig 2 shows the order of stitching.

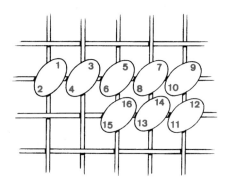

Fig 2 Tent stitch – order of stitching.

BASKETWEAVE STITCH

Basketweave is for backgrounds and large areas of colour. It is worked in diagonal rows and, as a result, puts less pressure on the canvas, so distortion is less severe. Fig 3 shows the order of stitching. The name 'basketweave' comes from the woven pattern that is created on the back of the canvas when this stitch is used. You will need to take care when starting new lengths of wool: try to end 'mid-row' so that it is easy to tell in which direction you were travelling. If you do two 'down' rows instead of one 'down' and one 'up', you will end up with a slight diagonal ridge.

Both types of stitch are worked using a stabbing rather than a sewing motion. Whichever type of stitch you use, make sure that all stitches over the whole design lie in the same direction.

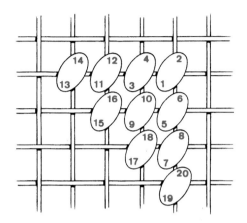

Fig 3 Basketweave stitch – order of stitching.

USING THE CHARTS

The instructions for each carpet design give all the necessary information. The colour key in each case lists the shades used in the design, giving the Appleton's shade numbers (for an exact match with the carpet shown) together with my own description of each shade. If you decide to use thread other than Appleton's, then by using these descriptions and consulting the colour photo of the finished carpet, you should be able to find a close match.

The design size is given for each carpet when worked on 18 count canvas. These are the maximum dimensions of the design *before* it is hemmed or finished in any way. All measurements are given in imperial with metric equivalents, rounded to the nearest half-centimetre for simplicity. You must stick to one or the other. (*See* page 132 for an exact metric conversion table.)

The stitch count is given next. This is another way of describing the carpet's eventual size. It is really only important if you intend to work the design on a canvas count other than 18, and want to work out what the carpet's size will be. Refer back to the section on canvas in the Essential Equipment chapter (pages 4–5) for how to do this. Whichever count of canvas you are using, remember that one square on a chart always equals one stitch.

The third set of measurements given is the size of canvas needed, and I have allowed a margin of 2in (5cm) spare canvas on each side (to make blocking and finishing easier). If you want to fix your canvas to a frame, one of these measurements will have to be altered to match the width of your frame, plus at least 1in (2.5cm) to allow you to attach it to the roller bars.

The method of working for each design is quite detailed, and I have tried to make it as easy as possible to work even the most complicated designs in simple, logical steps. Where a chart has been split over two or three pages, a repeated strip is indicated. Take care only to stitch these rows once. The small arrowhead indicates the centre of each side.

The colours used in printing each chart are not meant to be an exact match to those on the actual carpet. To make it easier to see the difference between close shades of one colour, an exaggerated differentiation in shade is shown on the charts.

FINISHING

Having spent hours painstakingly making your miniature carpet, it is very tempting to rush this part in order to see the finished product in place. Try to resist this temptation! If you do not spend some time finishing off properly, you could spoil an otherwise perfect piece of needlework.

The first thing to do is to check carefully to make sure that no stitches have been missed. Then trim any loose threads on the reverse side to make it as flat as possible when finished.

The carpet can be washed if need be. Make sure that you use cool water so that unstable dyes do not run, and use soap flakes or special needlework detergent. Move the canvas about in the water, but do not rub it. Rinse well in cold water, then roll it up in a towel and press (don't wring) the water out. Open the carpet out flat on the towel, placing another towel on top, weigh it down to keep flat and leave to dry off.

BLOCKING

Blocking will only need to be done if you have not used a frame and the canvas has pulled out of shape. You will need a piece of fibreboard or plywood large enough to take the canvas, several sheets of blotting paper or sheeting, a ruler or set square and some drawing pins. Blocking should be done while the canvas is damp.

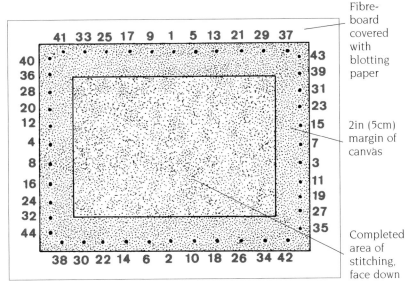

Fibre-board covered with blotting paper

2in (5cm) margin of canvas

Completed area of stitching, face down

Fig 4 Blocking the canvas – pinning order.

First remove the masking tape that bound the edges of the canvas and mark the centres of each side lightly with a pencil. Place the canvas face down onto the board, which should be generously covered with blotting paper or sheeting. Start to pin around the edges of the canvas in the order indicated in Fig 4, pulling the canvas square as you go, and checking with the set square or ruler that the edges are straight. Place pins about every ½in (1.5cm). Spray the canvas thoroughly with water once the pinning out is completed, then put the blocked canvas somewhere flat for two to three days to dry completely. If the canvas is very distorted, it might not be possible to get it square the first time and you might have to repeat the process.

Once the carpet is completely dry and square, trim away the excess canvas to ½in (1.5cm) all round, ready for hemming.

HEMMING

Hemming the carpet serves two functions: it gives a neat appearance to the edge, and keeps the unworked canvas securely folded to the back of the work.

Rectangular shapes

Most of the carpets presented in this book are rectangular, and these are the easiest to deal with. Fig 5 shows what needs to be done. Starting half way along one side, turn the canvas under so that the first row of 'empty' holes is along the edge of the carpet, and then oversew with a double thickness of wool in the needle, in the same shade as the final row of stitches. Make sure that each stitch begins in the same hole as the outermost line of tent stitches, and that it goes vertically through the two layers each time. This will give you the neatest edge. As you approach a corner, carefully fold down the adjoining edge and oversew around the corner through the two thicknesses, working the very

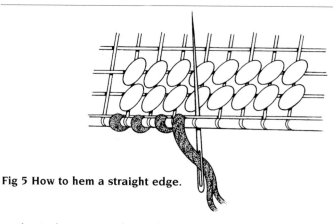

Fig 5 How to hem a straight edge.

end stitches twice through the same hole to make sure that the bare canvas is properly covered.

To start each length of thread, secure the end by running a few stitches through the back of the work near where you want to begin hemming. Finish off in the same way. Hemming like this should hold the unworked canvas securely to the back. If it still seems to stand proud, run a line of clear fabric glue along the rough edge and press down until it sticks.

Irregular shapes

Round and irregularly shaped carpets cannot be hemmed in this way because the finished edge does not run evenly along a row of holes. To finish these, trim the canvas as usual (to about ½in[1.5cm] all round). Spread fabric glue over all the unworked canvas and allow to dry thoroughly. Then, referring to Fig 6, snip the canvas up to the stitching at short intervals around concave curves, and cut V-shapes out along convex ones. Dab fabric glue along the cuts again if necessary to prevent unravelling, then fold each 'tab' to the reverse side, leaving no bare canvas showing from the front or edge. Run your nail along the edge to press the tab into position, then secure it in place with a couple of stitches using strong thread. Do small sections at a time to achieve a smooth outline.

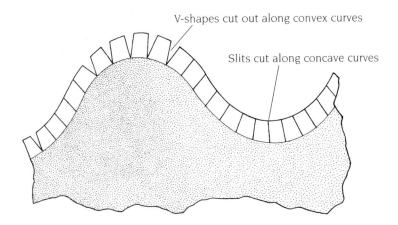

V-shapes cut out along convex curves

Slits cut along concave curves

Fig 6 Trimming the canvas for a curved edge.

The method for a carpet as oddly shaped as the tiger skin (page 65) is different again. After all the stitching is completed, run a good line of fabric glue around the edge of the stitching, overlapping onto the unworked canvas. Leave to dry thoroughly, then, with a sharp pair of scissors, carefully cut away all the bare canvas right up to the stitching. You will need to be feeling brave to do this, but the glue will work, and the tight curves (around the paws of the tiger, for instance) will be much flatter and neater if dealt with in this way.

To simulate the 'skin' of the tiger, you will need a piece of interfacing (*see* page 19). This is usually sold as a white fabric, so to dye it to the beige shade that you need, pour some freshly brewed tea into a bowl. Dip the fabric into the tea for about a minute until it has absorbed the colour sufficiently and leave to dry completely. Run a generous band of fabric glue around the edge of the stitched carpet, and also dot glue over the underside of the main body area. Place the carpet onto the fabric and press together firmly. Once the glue has dried, trim away the excess fabric so that it only just shows around the edge of the stitching.

ALTERNATIVE FINISHES

There are several other ways of finishing a carpet. For example, the edges could be trimmed, turned under and the unworked canvas slip-stitched to the back of the work.

Alternatively, the edges could be held in place with strips of Vilene or Wundaweb. Vilene is a non-woven fabric similar to felt, but much thinner, used as an interfacing in dressmaking. It is available in three weights – light, medium and heavy – and two versions – standard or iron-on – and is usually sold by the metre in haberdashery departments or needlework shops. For the skin backing of the tiger rug on page 65, I used the standard type of Vilene and glued it in place. Had I used the iron-on type, the edges would have curled up and stuck to the stitching around the edge, spoiling the effect. Wundaweb is a similar fabric, always iron-on and sold in narrow strips. It will stick a turned-up piece of fabric to an adjoining piece, avoiding the need to stitch a hem. This, or iron-on Vilene, would be best for neatening the reverse of carpets other than the tiger skin.

If you are sure you will not change your mind, you could even stick the carpet directly to the floor of your dolls' house using double-sided tape. This is also a good way to fix staircarpet. Even if you use stair rods to hold the carpet down, a narrow strip of tape here and there will help keep it flat on the treads.

FRINGING

'Real' carpets often have fringed ends. This is a way of decoratively tying the ends of the warp threads after a carpet has been cut from the loom, but it can easily be achieved on miniature carpets as well.

Hem the two long sides of the carpet by your chosen method. Trim the bare canvas from these hemmed sides as close as possible to the stitching, to cut down the bulk at the corners. The two short sides can then be dealt with using fringing stitch, which is shown in Fig 7. Use perle cotton or thin crochet cotton to work the fringe, in a neutral shade. You will need approximately one yard of cotton for every inch of fringing (or one metre for every 2.5cm). Cotton, being thinner than wool, gives a flatter, more realistic look to the fringe. If you place a lollipop stick or a pencil in the loops as you make them, they will all be the same size when completed. Cut the loops when the whole carpet is finished.

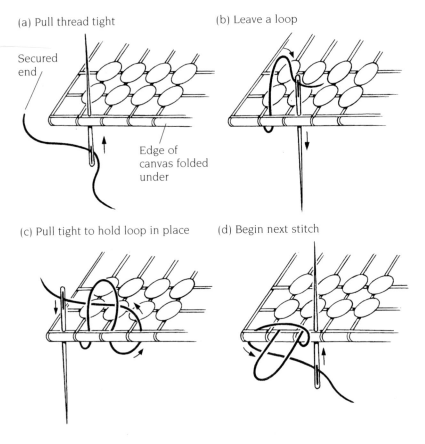

(a) Pull thread tight

Secured
end

Edge of
canvas folded
under

(b) Leave a loop

(c) Pull tight to hold loop in place

(d) Begin next stitch

Fig 7 Fringing stitch.

Planning your own Designs

You may find that the designs offered in this book are not exactly what you want, or, having tried some out, you may want to move on. What if you like the middle of one design, but not the border, and the colour scheme does not suit your dolls' house? The answer is to design your own, either incorporating elements from these designs, or designing from scratch. This is really not difficult to achieve. All you need is some graph paper (squared tracing paper in different counts is also available) and a handful of coloured pencils.

If you are feeling adventurous, a cross stitch software package for a PC might be the next stage up. There are several on the market now, and they vary enormously in price and quality. If you are interested in investing in one, send off for a sample disk first to be sure that you are getting the correct package for your needs.

COLOUR

The main ingredient of a successful design is colour. In miniature needlework, the trick is to give the effect of a complicated design, but without using as many shades as in the full-size version. If you are just starting out, stick to five or six colours per design at the most – one very light, one very dark, and the rest in between. Also, the finished carpet needs to be toned down with more grey shades than the real thing, so that it does not jump out at you visually when placed in the dolls' house. Shade cards are very useful when designing as you can play around with unusual colour combinations. As an alternative, when in a shop, hold all the colours you are thinking of buying in one hand, in natural light if possible, to get an idea of their compatibility. If your carpet is to have large, plain areas of colour, always buy a shade or two lighter than you think, as large areas seem to end up looking denser in tone when finished.

The effect colours have on each other is an area far too large to be covered in detail here. If you want to investigate colour theory in depth, I suggest you visit your local library (the art section of the children's library is often a good place to start). Fig 8 shows the three primary colours (yellow, blue and red), and their complementary colours (violet, orange and green). Primary colours are the fundamental colours, which cannot be obtained by mixing, but which can be combined to create other colours. The complementary colours of the primaries are their 'negatives' – when placed side by side they intensify each other by contrast.

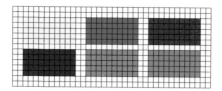

Fig 8 Primary and complementary colours.

This basic idea is central to designing with colour. So, if you want a strong colour to complement the green in your design, choose red. If you want dots of colour in a carpet of varying shades of blue, choose orange. Fig 9 gives examples, showing how the look of a design can change with different choices of colour. Notice how, depending where pairs of colour are placed in the design, certain areas can appear to advance or recede.

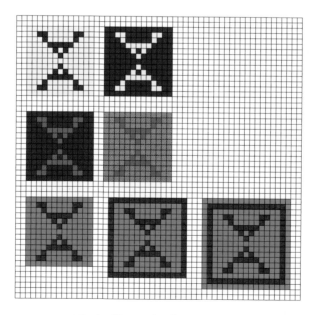

Fig 9 Effects of colour choices.

USING PATTERN REPEATS

All patterns are built up from small units. This is the best way to approach designing – think small, then let it grow! Fig 10 shows how this works in practice. A small flower motif is all that is needed as the basis for a design. Simply build it up and repeat it at intervals in different directions to obtain a border pattern or an all-over design for a larger carpet. Reflecting the motif across the horizontal and vertical axes gives you even more options.

Fig 10 Building pattern repeats.

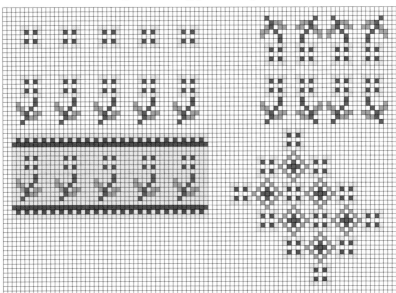

BORDERS

The finishing touch to almost every carpet in this book is its border. Even a narrow border of stripes using the main colours in the design can be eye-catching and effective. If you are designing with any sort of motif, however, you need to plan beforehand how you will tackle the corners so that the pattern flows. There are several ways of doing this, as shown in Fig 11. You can simply count out the border motifs from the centre of each side until you hit the corner, the position of which you have decided on earlier, and if the motifs meet at the corner in a jumble of pattern, so be it! Another way is to design a corner block motif, on a similar theme to the border pattern, and again count out the border motifs from the centre of each side of the carpet. This time they will seem to 'disappear' behind the corner motif, which will give a tidier finish to the design.

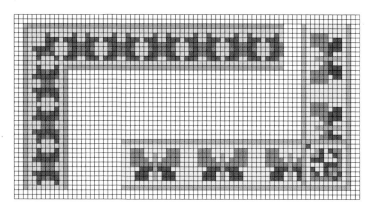

Fig 11 Planning borders and corners.

The best way to handle borders, however, is to calculate the size of central field available in multiples of border repeat, before designing the middle of the carpet. For instance, if the border motif is seven squares wide, with a blank square between each repeat, the inner border edge will need to be, say, 3 x 7-square border motifs (i.e. 21 squares), plus 2 x 1-square gaps, which is 23 squares length in total. (This will make the motifs touch at the inner border corners. If you want gaps at either end, you will need to add an equal amount of blank squares to both ends of each side.) The short side in this example is 2 x 7-square motifs plus a 1-square gap, which equals 15 squares. So the central area will be

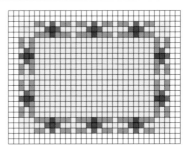

Fig 12 Calculating border motif repeats.

23 squares long and 15 squares wide. See Fig 12 for an illustration of this example.

If you use this method and design your border first, even if it is only 'border blocks' of colour with no detail in as yet, you will not have the problem of designing a brilliant border later, only to find that it does not fit because the multiples are wrong. You can then choose how to deal with the corners of the border, using either of the methods outlined earlier.

INSPIRATION

To begin designing you just need to get a few coloured pencils in your hand and have a go. Colour in a few squares, make a pattern, add a few highlights with a light and a dark shade, and you have a design! It's as simple as that. Once you begin to look around, it is amazing where you can find ideas for carpets. There are the really obvious places, of course, such as carpet catalogues, available from furniture showrooms. Many designs for soft furnishings such as fabric or wallpaper, or even tiles, can also easily be translated into carpets. Wrapping paper is another good design source. Often, the best ideas come from nature. A dramatic landscape, or a bunch of flowers, for example, can easily get your imagination going once you learn to tune in to the possibilities. If you can, keep a folder of ideas and notes of sources to refer to later.

General
▪ Designs ▪

▪ 1 ▪
Medallion design

Difficulty rating: ★
Design size: 6½ x 5in (16.5 x 13cm)
Stitch count: 119 x 89 stitches
Size of canvas needed: 10½ x 9in (26.5 x 23cm)

INTRODUCTION

This was the very first carpet I ever designed. I had just bought my large, eight-room dolls' house and it looked so bare inside that I felt I had to soften it as a matter of urgency! There is a good deal of solid maroon background in this design (almost three whole skeins), so make sure that you buy enough in one go to complete the design, as batch shades vary.

METHOD

Starting in the centre, work the maroon hearts and curls, then the green flowers. Carefully count out the green lozenge shape, and fill in the relevant areas with blue-grey and peach, using basketweave stitch for each. From the outermost points of the lozenge, work out the maximum dimensions of the plain maroon background and work the outer line only, then work the hearts in each corner. Fill in the maroon area using basketweave stitch.

Count out the width of the border and work two rows of maroon, adding the two-stitch 'bars' as you go. Next, work the green U-shapes, alternating them upwards and downwards

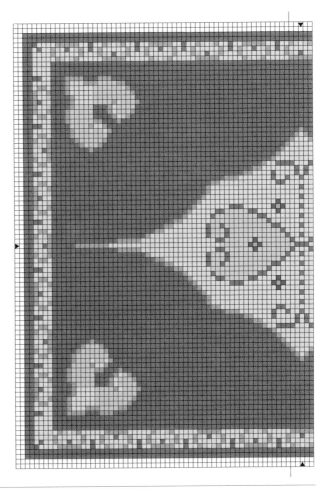

around the design. Add the highlights with blue-grey and maroon, and finish off by filling in the background with peach.

Medallion Design

	886	Pale blue-grey		833	Dark grass green
	706	Pale peach		148	Maroon
	831	Medium green			

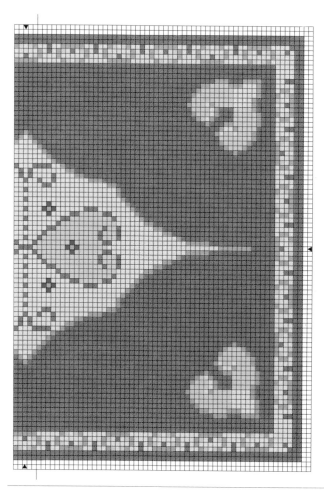

▪ 2 ▪
Circular
scene

Difficulty rating: ★★
Design size: 4 x 4in (10 x 10cm)
Stitch count: 69 x 69 stitches
Size of canvas needed: 8 x 8in (20 x 20cm)

INTRODUCTION

This summer scene of birds and cherries is an example of how one idea can be adapted to fit in with another. I began by wanting a circular design and this one worked well – on paper. Once stitched, however, the small circle proved very difficult to finish off neatly, so I abandoned the round carpet idea on this occasion and enclosed it in a square instead.

Although the key lists twelve shades of wool for this carpet, most of them are only used in very small quantities. So if you have oddments left over from other projects, this is an ideal way to use them up. The only colours which you will need in any quantity at all are the two shades of blue.

METHOD

Start in the centre of the design and work the larger bird, then the smaller, perching one. With medium brown, work all the branches, highlighting with the dark brown. Next, work the cherries. To place all the leaves, it is easiest to work all the dark green veins first, then the pale green bodies of the leaves. The circle of china blue can then be worked, and the triangular corners. This makes it clear which areas need to be filled in with sky blue in basketweave stitch, and saves on counting. Finally, work a row of china blue to finish off the design.

Circular scene

▓	998	Charcoal	░	461	Sky blue
▓	187	Dark brown	▓	745	China blue
▓	185	Medium brown	▓	605	Purple
░	183	Beige	▓	755	Rose pink
▓	646	Dark green	░	602	Pale purple
░	642	Pale green	▓	948	Cherry

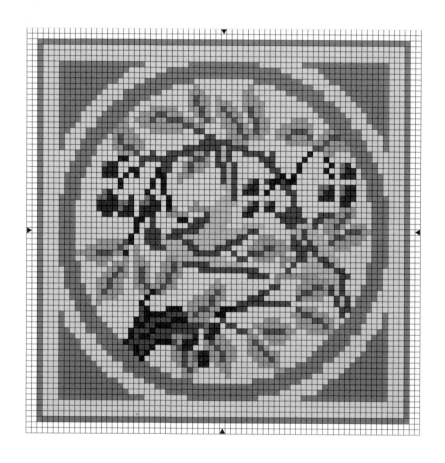

■ 3 ■
All-over leaf design

Difficulty rating: ★★
Design size: 4½ x 6¾in (11.5 x 17cm)
Stitch count: 80 x 122 stitches
Size of canvas needed: 8½ x 10¾in (21.5 x 27cm)

INTRODUCTION

The idea for the pattern of this all-over design came from the wallpaper in a friend's house, a sweet wrapper and some jewellery. If anyone can identify which of these became which parts of the design, I should offer a prize! It just goes to show that inspiration can come from the most unlikely sources: you just need to keep your eyes open.

METHOD

Begin by working the burgundy trellis and two rows of border. Next work the gold motifs, highlighting with hazel brown. In the areas of trellis that remain, work the stems in hazel brown, followed by the moss green leaf centres and finishing off with dark chestnut brown for the rest of the leaf shapes. Fill in the whole of the carpet background with ecru in basketweave stitch, completing the carpet with two rows of dark chestnut brown for the outermost border.

This all-over repeating pattern can easily be extended if you wish to make a much larger carpet. Simply continue with the wavy burgundy lines until you reach the required size, before filling in the detail.

All-over leaf design

■	128	Dark chestnut brown
■	904	Hazel brown
▨	843	Gold
□	882	Ecru
■	356	Moss green
■	226	Burgundy

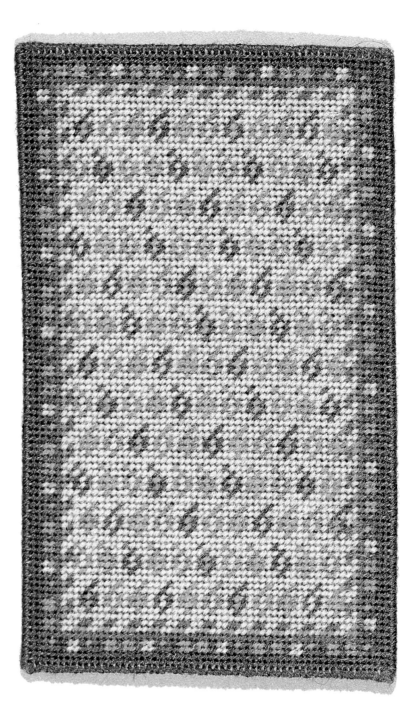

∎ 4 ∎
Paisley pattern

Difficulty rating: ★★
Design size: 5¼ x 3½in (13 x 9cm)
Stitch count: 94 x 58 stitches
Size of canvas needed: 9¼ x 7½in (23.5 x 19cm)

INTRODUCTION

The origin of the well-known paisley pattern is an interesting one. In the early 1800s patterned shawls, which were handmade from the fleece of goats from the Kashmir area, began to be imported from India to Britain. These shawls proved to be so popular that machine-made ones were manufactured at Paisley in Scotland to try to satisfy the huge demand. The curvilinear designs used on the shawls derived originally from Mughal art, the most usual being the 'comma' shape which we have come to know as 'paisley pattern'. This is still a very popular motif, appearing on clothing as well as household fabrics. This carpet would suit any style of house from the 1820s to the present day.

METHOD

This deceptively simple design calls for careful counting, so beware! Begin in the centre of the design using light turquoise, and count out the paisley pattern centres. Do the same using fawn in between the turquoise. Then start in one corner of the carpet and work diagonal rows of paisley shapes, taking note that one row will point to the left and the next to the right, across the design. Continue in sequence with pale charcoal, gunmetal grey and cinnamon until all the paisley pattern is completed. Work the two-tone, offset edging to the border, then one row of cinnamon, before filling in all the central field's background with fawn.

For the border, work the two rows of pale charcoal with two-stitch 'bars' inwards in one go. Add the light turquoise dots, then the other colours in sequence around the border, completing the design.

Paisley pattern

	964	Gunmetal grey
	967	Pale charcoal
	697	Cinnamon
	764	Biscuit brown
	984	Fawn
	481	Light turquoise

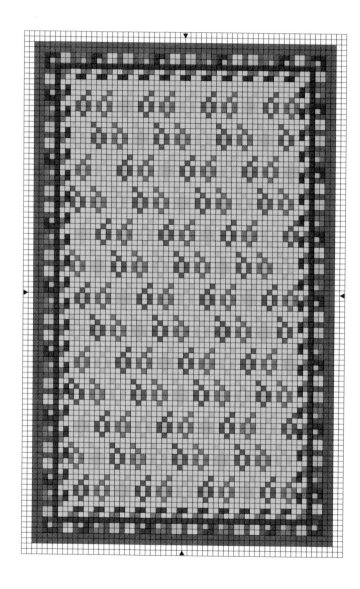

▪ 5 ▪
Traditional abstract design

Difficulty rating: ★★
Design size: 6 x 4¼in (15 x 11cm)
Stitch count: 111 x 77 stitches
Size of canvas needed: 10 x 8¼in (25.5 x 21cm)

INTRODUCTION

The pattern on some Victorian floor tiles gave me the basis for this design. I liked the mix of colours and adapted the tile effect for the ends of the central field, juxtaposing that with the flowing pattern of the border. If you look closely, you will see that the motif used in the border is taken from part of the carpet's central pattern, then simply repeated all the way round.

METHOD

Work the centre cross in cinnamon, then, using olive green, work the rest of the central motif's framework. Working all of the green in one go makes it much simpler to place the other dots of colour in this design. After the olive, use cinnamon again, then highlight with the two paler greens. Outline this hexagonal area with cinnamon and olive green, then fill in the background with putty grey using basketweave stitch. Next work the two shaded green areas at each end of the carpet's main field. After that, work the three-row border to the main field, leaving only the chequered area to be worked. This is best done by placing the olive dots first, then joining these up with cinnamon and working the pale olive areas last. Again, fill in the background with putty grey.

For the border, count the width and work one row of cinnamon, then work out the placing of the centre lines for each motif in light grey-green before adding the other colours, until the individual motifs join up to make a flowing border pattern. Finally work the outer border stripes, finishing with two rows of olive green.

Traditional abstract design

■	697	Cinnamon
□	987	Putty grey
▨	351	Light grey-green
■	343	Pale olive green
■	245	Olive green

Functional
▪ Carpets ▪

▪6▪
Classic doormat

Difficulty rating: ★
Design size: 4 x 2½in (10 x 6.5cm)
Stitch count: 73 x 43 stitches
Size of canvas needed: 8 x 6½in (20 x 16.5cm)

INTRODUCTION

This small, classical design works well as a doormat in a hallway of black and white tiles. It might be tiny, but it knows its own importance! The colours can easily be changed to match any colour scheme: pink and maroon would look good, or pale green and dark brown. The main motif could also be repeated lengthways several times for a hallway runner, with the same border stitched around the whole carpet once it has reached the desired size.

METHOD

Begin by working the central diamond-shaped motif in charcoal. Working outwards, continue with the motifs at both ends. Count around the border for the alternate-stitch pattern, working the solid line of charcoal last. Fill in with the cream, using basketweave stitch.

Classic doormat

	877	Cream
	998	Charcoal

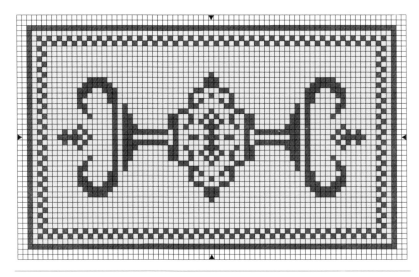

▪ 7 ▪
Bathmat with lettering

Difficulty rating: ★
Design size: 4¼ x 3in (10.5 x 7.5cm)
Stitch count: 76 x 52 stitches
Size of canvas needed: 8 x 7in (20 x 18cm)

INTRODUCTION

This small design can be finished in a few hours, and makes a good project for beginners. Alter the colours to suit your own bathroom colour scheme if you wish.

METHOD

Begin by working the lettering and inner border in purple, then fill in the background around the lettering with pale lavender. Still using lavender, work the daisy shapes. Work the off-white 'lace' surrounding the daisies. It is simpler if you work the very outside wavy line first, then you can just 'colour in' the rest. Next work the plain outer pale lavender area, completing the carpet with a final row of purple.

Bathmat with lettering

	884	Pale lavender
	605	Purple
	881	Off-white

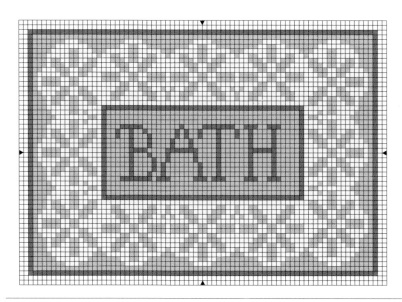

■ 8 ■
Rose repeat staircarpet

Difficulty rating: ★★
Design size: 1¼ x 20in (3 x 51cm)
Stitch count: 23 x 360 stitches
Size of canvas needed: 5¼ x 24in (13 x 61cm)

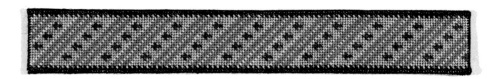

INTRODUCTION

Staircarpets are easy to do as the designs are simple and grow quickly. Before you start, work out how long the carpet needs to be. This is simple if your dolls' house staircase is removable, but often the hallway is wallpapered and painted before thoughts of a staircarpet come to mind. This makes things a little trickier, but not impossible. Whether the staircase can be removed or not, I have found that the best way to measure the distance up a flight of stairs is to cut a long, narrow strip of canvas and simply bend it along the length of the staircase. Using canvas rather than paper avoids the need to make an allowance later for the stiffness of the canvas as it bends over the treads. It helps to secure the canvas strip temporarily with a piece of masking tape, to hold it in place while you 'walk' the canvas up the stairs. Use a couple of rulers to poke it right into the back of each tread.

If you want to carpet several flights of stairs, including the landings, make a separate strip for each flight, with another piece for the landing. It would be far too difficult to try to work several flights and landings all in one piece.

These staircarpets are designed to allow a small amount of woodwork to show on either side of the carpet. This will give you space to fix stair rods. To make the carpet wider, however, a simple way would be to pick out colours from the main body of the design and work single-row stripes of stitches up each side. Make sure that you work a row of the same colour on both sides for balance. Also remember to allow for the fact that, when the carpet is hemmed, it will end up very slightly wider.

As these designs are so narrow, and the length will vary according to the size of your staircase, it is not as important as usual to begin in the exact centre of the design. If you are using a frame, the length of canvas you have to cut will probably have to be wound round the frame rollers quite a bit before becoming taut. As long as you start roughly in the centre of the canvas that is visible on the prepared frame, however, that will be fine. Work each frame width completely before moving on to the next section; this will help prevent the canvas from warping.

The charts which follow show enough of the pattern to include several repeats. Simply keep going along the same lines until you have reached the length you need.

METHOD

Work the baby pink diagonals first, then the dark olive green edging. Take great care over the 'castellations' where they intersect with the pink diagonal lines – do not inadvertently make the carpet wider than it should be! Next work the flowers, followed by the leaves, and the pale green background. Finally work the blush pink of the plain bands.

Rose repeat staircarpet

	754	Blush pink
	756	Deep rose
	541	Pale leaf green
	548	Dark olive green
	544	Medium leaf green
	751	Baby pink

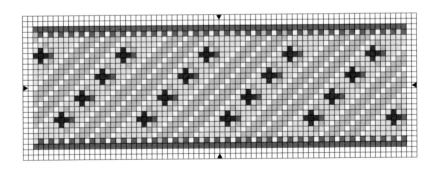

▪ 9 ▪
Olive repeat staircarpet

Difficulty rating: ★★
Design size: 1½ x 20in (4 x 51cm)
Stitch count: 26 x 360 stitches
Size of canvas needed: 5½ x 24in (14 x 61cm)

METHOD

Work the mulberry diamonds up the centre first, then fill these in with the dark marine blue and gunmetal grey. Work the outer mulberry borders next, filling in with the blue. Edge the design with bitter chocolate, and finish off by working the drab green main background in basketweave stitch. (*See* pages 54–55 for general instructions on staircarpets.)

Olive repeat staircarpet

	964	Gunmetal grey
	714	Mulberry
	586	Bitter chocolate
	335	Drab green
	326	Dark marine blue

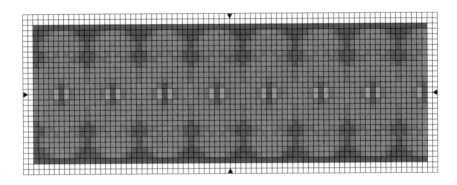

Modern
▪ Designs ▪

▪ 10 ▪
Art Deco style

Difficulty rating: ★
Design size: 5 x 3½in (12.5 x 9cm)
Stitch count: 92 x 64 stitches
Size of canvas needed: 9 x 7½in (23 x 19cm)

INTRODUCTION

I wanted to include some more modern designs, because I feel that those with dolls' houses of more recent styles often lose out. Not everyone wants to have a vaguely Victorian-style house, and this carpet is especially for anyone with a yearning to attempt an abstract design from the Art Deco era. It echoes the clean lines and geometric shapes of the 1930s furniture which is becoming increasingly popular – in the dolls' house world as well as the real one!

METHOD

Start in the centre by working the blue diagonal lines. This will give you a reference point for counting out the other shapes.

Although this design looks simple, it is easy to miscount with such gaps between the main areas of colour. Work the long line of tomato red next, followed by the pale tangerine corner shape. Count out the outline of the tomato red circle, then colour it in. From the edge of the circle, count out to the stripey line and work each diagonal part of the stripe. Lastly, fill in all the background with stone, using basketweave stitch. As the design has such a large plain background area, it is important to use basketweave stitch for this part. It will ensure that the canvas threads are covered properly and will give an evenness to the whole carpet.

Art Deco style

	866	Tomato red
	473	Pale tangerine
	981	Stone
	853	Winchester blue
	998	Charcoal

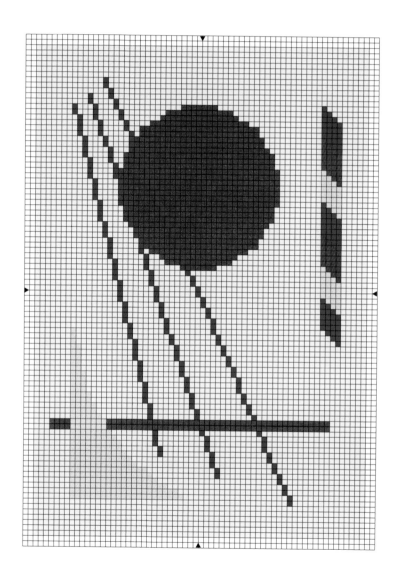

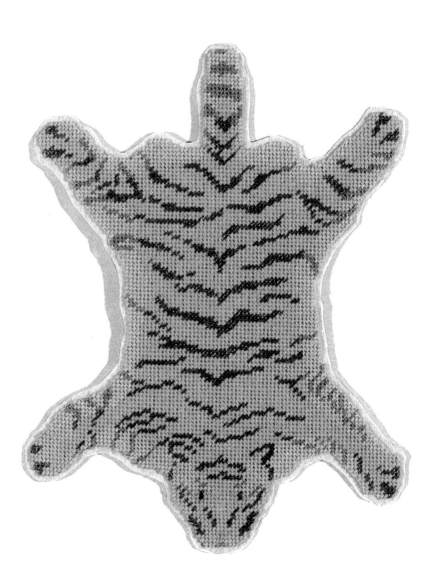

▪ 11 ▪
Tiger skin rug

Difficulty rating: ★★
Design size: 7 x 5½in (18 x 14cm)
Stitch count: 124 x 96 stitches
Size of canvas needed: 11 x 9½in (28 x 24cm)

INTRODUCTION

This is a fun design, and is quite quick to do. I sketched the design after looking at a real tiger skin. The body seems surprisingly fat, but this is how it really looked!

As this carpet has an uneven edge to it, it cannot be hemmed in the usual way. Special finishing instructions are given on page 18.

METHOD

Starting in the centre, work all the dark brown stripes over the whole design. Then work all the outer stripes with light brown. Work the eyes and nose next. Using tangerine, carefully count around the outline of the main part of the tiger skin. This will give you a thin-looking tiger, which should be filled in next using basketweave stitch. Lastly, count out the outer edge of the skin using the mustard shade, and fill in these areas to complete the design.

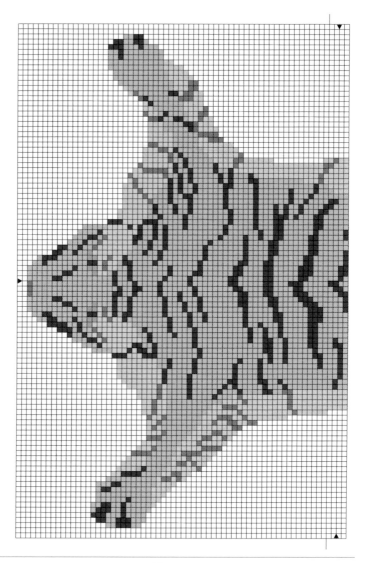

Tiger skin rug

	187	Dark brown		693	Mustard
	474	Tangerine		332	Sage green
	184	Light brown		754	Blush pink

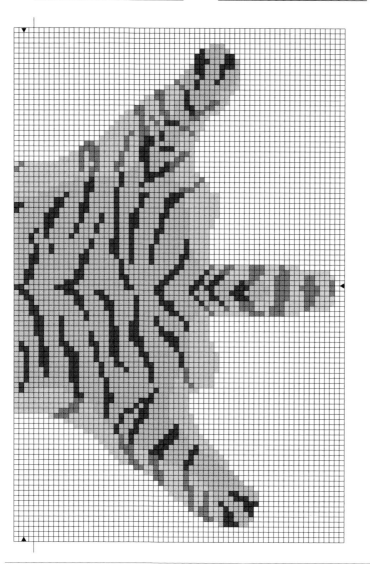

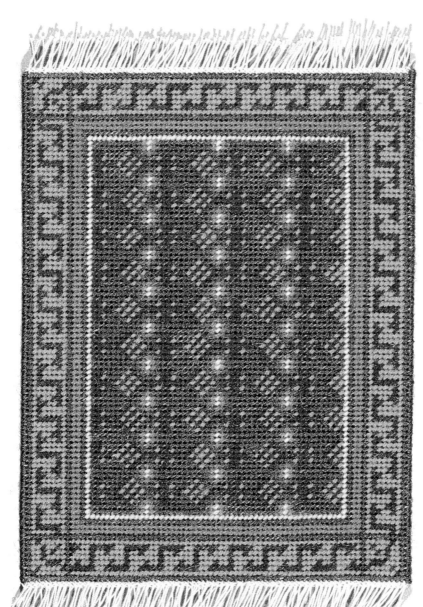

▪ 12 ▪
Geometric repeat

Difficulty rating: ★★
Design size: 4¼ x 5½in (11 x 14cm)
Stitch count: 77 x 98 stitches
Size of canvas needed: 8¼ x 9½in (20 x 24cm)

INTRODUCTION

This design has a warm, Christmassy feel to it. The lilac shades add depth to the pattern, while the dark green and maroon shades make it appear rich and expensive. This is not a design for a 'poor' dolls' house! It would look good in a cluttered study full of dusty books, with treasures collected from exotic corners of the world displayed around the room.

METHOD

Starting at the centre, work the dark grass green diamond and trellis pattern first. Using the lilac shades, work the graduated diamonds, doing the ecru centres last. Next work the maroon crosses and their sage green corners. For the chequered diamonds, take great care over the placing of the maroon and sage green stitches, as they alternate down the design as well as across it.

When the main area of the carpet is complete, work the solid border stripes, then the outer dark grass green border line. Leave the Greek key design area to be filled in last – working the maroon pattern before completing the background.

Geometric repeat

■	148	Maroon
□	882	Ecru
▨	102	Pale lilac
■	104	Dark lilac
■	833	Dark grass green
▨	332	Sage green

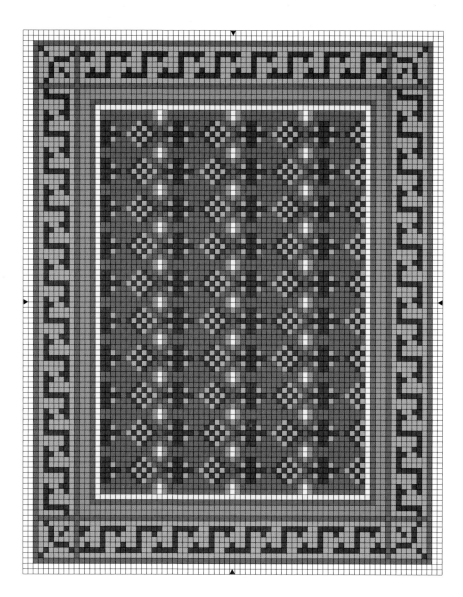

▪ 13 ▪
Asymmetrical repeat

Difficulty rating: ★★
Design size: 5 x 6¾in (13 x 17cm)
Stitch count: 89 x 123 stitches
Size of canvas needed: 9 x 10¾in (23 x 27cm)

INTRODUCTION
This type of carpet would look quite at home in anything from a Victorian-style house right up to a very modern one. The design is timeless – small pattern blocks are fitted together for a patchwork effect. The use of a limited colour palette helps bind the different patterns together, giving a busy but co-ordinated look to the carpet.

METHOD
Starting at the centre, count out the dark blue dividing lines for the boxes. After that, this carpet can be worked as if it is lots of mini carpets put together. Each small area is worked by filling in the main area colour, then the highlights, with the background filled in last. If

you work each matching pair of motifs at once, it will save considerable time as you will not have to re-thread the needle so often.

When all the central area has been completed, work the outermost blue border line, then the corner motifs, and fill in with the blue and mustard crosses. Finally work the border background using dark chestnut brown.

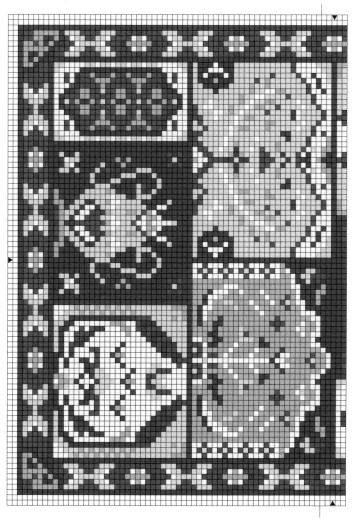

Asymmetrical repeat

■	128	Dark chestnut brown	▨	922	Airforce blue
▨	693	Mustard	■	929	Dark blue
□	981	Stone			

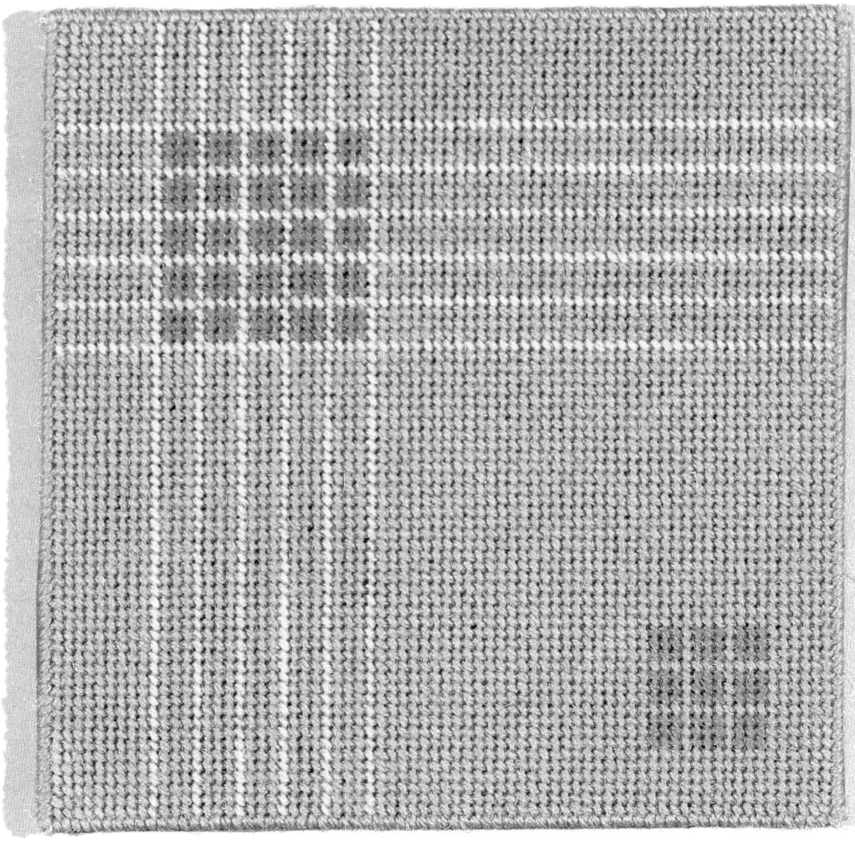

▪ 14 ▪
After Charles Rennie Mackintosh

Difficulty rating: ★
Design size: 4 x 4in (10 x 10cm)
Stitch count: 72 x 72 stitches
Size of canvas needed: 8 x 8in (20 x 20cm)

INTRODUCTION

This stark design is in the style of Charles Rennie Mackintosh, who was an architect and designer of the Glasgow school at the turn of the century.

The design could be repeated as 'blocks' to make a larger square carpet, turning the design to obtain different effects. You could also join several pattern repeats together in a line to make a hall carpet.

METHOD

Work the lines of cream first, then fill in the large blue square. Count out the maximum dimensions and work a row of fawn, then work the smaller blue square before filling in all of the remaining carpet in fawn, using basketweave stitch.

After Charles Rennie Mackintosh

	984	Fawn
	877	Cream
	742	Wedgwood blue

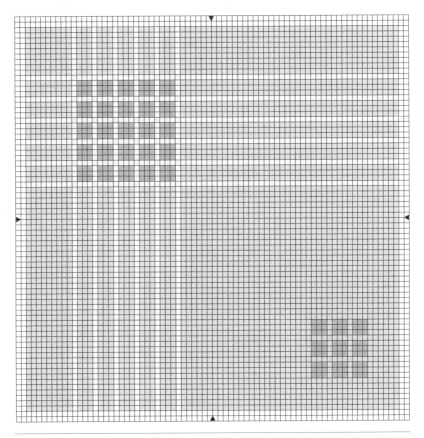

Traditional
■ Designs ■

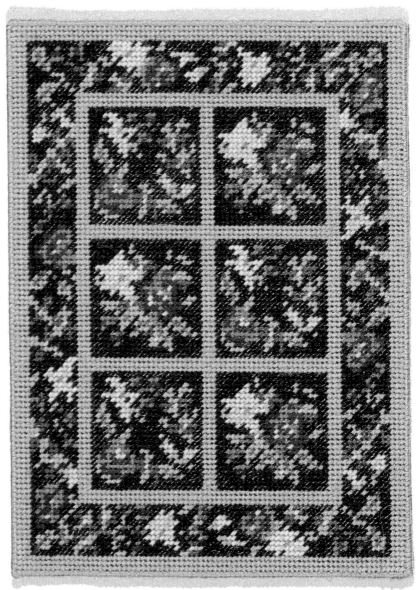

▪ 15 ▪
Berlin woolwork style

Difficulty rating: ★★★
Design size: 6 x 4½in (15 x 11.5cm)
Stitch count: 107 x 81 stitches
Size of canvas needed: 10 x 8½in (25.5 x 21.5cm)

INTRODUCTION

Berlin woolwork was a type of embroidery which became enormously popular in the 1830s. It derived its name from the German city of Berlin, and the designs were imported from there to Britain. At first only the paper charts were imported, and they were actually very similar to the charts shown in this book – except that each one was coloured by hand. As this was so labour intensive, manufacturers soon began to print the design directly onto the canvas. The designs could be worked either in tent stitch or cross stitch, sometimes using beads for added detail. Berlin woolwork designs tend to be rather gaudy, but are always cheerful.

METHOD

The centre six squares of this carpet consist of two motifs repeated three times each. If you work, for example, all the dark lilac areas for one motif at the same time, you will not need to re-thread your needle so often.

Begin with the dull turquoise and work the six central squares, then highlight the inside of each square with light green. Work each of the floral motifs completely three times across the carpet before working the background to these areas. Next highlight the outside edge of the turquoise squares and, with light green, count the width of the floral border before working a second row of light green.

Starting in one corner, fill in the border with flowers. For this part of the carpet it will probably not help to do, say, all the green in one go, as the margin for error is considerable. Check often that you are following the chart accurately. When all the flower border is completed, fill in the background as before. Finally outline with one row of dull turquoise and another of light green.

Berlin woolwork style

▨	998	Charcoal	▨	546	Dark leaf green
▨	143	Dusty pink	▨	522	Dull turquoise
▮	505	Rich brick red	▨	886	Pale blue-grey
▢	841	Palest lemon	▮	104	Dark lilac
▨	542	Light green			

▪ 16 ▪
Italian style

Difficulty rating: ★★
Design size: 6 x 6in (15 x 15cm)
Stitch count: 105 x 105 stitches
Size of canvas needed: 10 x 10in (25.5 x 25.5cm)

INTRODUCTION

Squares and straight lines make up this formal Italianate carpet in shades of blue, rose and brown. The shades of brown complement the colours in mahogany very well, so the carpet can enhance any room containing fine furniture which you want to show off to best effect. I designed this one to go in the music room of my Georgian dolls' house, and I am very pleased with the final result.

METHOD

Using biscuit brown, begin with the fleur-de-lys design in the central field, adding the pale beige and brown highlights next. Work the three-line border to this area before filling in the pale

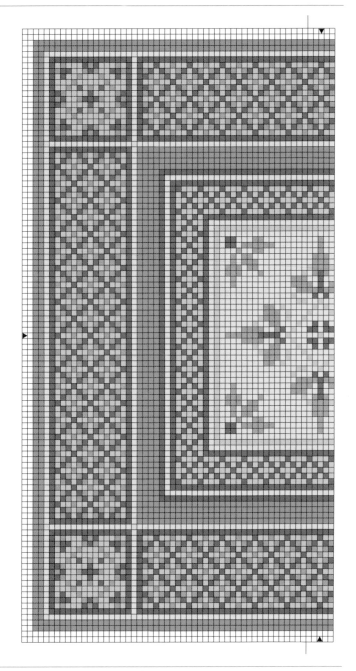

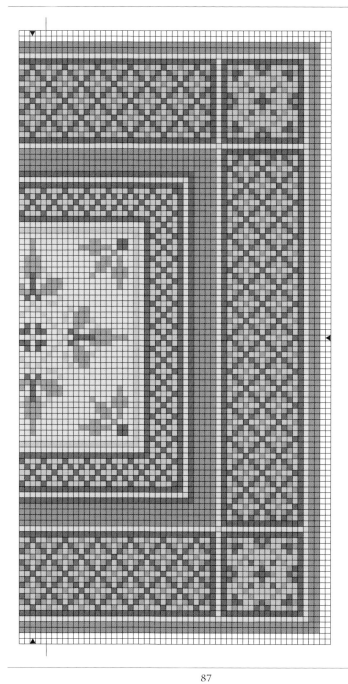

blue background. Count out the width of the first chequered border stripe with the dark biscuit brown, then zigzag across it, still with the same colour, to make the chequered pattern. Fill in the background with pale beige.

Work the straight lines and wide, dull rose pink border next, then count out the wide chequered border and corner squares using pale blue. Line each square or rectangular border area with dark biscuit brown, then begin to fill in the pattern. It is easiest on the eye to work the dark biscuit brown first, and to fill in the background with pale beige last. The corners should all be worked in the same order of dark biscuit brown, biscuit brown, then pale beige. Finally, work two rows of dull rose pink around the whole carpet to complete it.

Italian style

■	767	Dark biscuit brown
■	764	Biscuit brown
■	761	Pale beige
■	741	Pale blue
■	144	Dull rose pink

▪ 17 ▪
Regency style

Difficulty rating:★★★
Design size: 8½ x 6½in (21.5 x 16.5cm)
Stitch count: 150 x 118 stitches
Size of canvas needed: 12½ x 10½in (32 x 26.5cm)

INTRODUCTION

I designed this oval carpet specifically to complement the yellow colourway of the 'print room' wallpaper which is widely available from dolls' house stockists. The carpet has an elegant feel to it, and sets off a Georgian room perfectly. The central part of the design is abstract, and contrasts well with the strong, straight lines of the shaded yellow and orange background.

METHOD

Begin by working the centre oval in pale tangerine, then work the dark steel grey abstract areas. Work the silver areas next, and finally the gunmetal grey. Then count out to the ring of interlaced

loops and, working with gunmetal grey, complete in either direction, working the winged motifs at either end of the carpet last. Highlight with the dark steel grey and silver where necessary.

To work the yellow sunburst pattern, it is best to outline each area of colour as you go, and 'colour in' each section in turn before moving on to the next. To prevent the canvas from warping, move in a continuous sweep around the design rather than working all of a colour in one go.

For instructions on how to finish round and irregularly shaped carpets, see page 17.

Regency style

	964	Gunmetal grey
	966	Dark steel grey
	473	Pale tangerine
	474	Tangerine
	471	Pale lemon
	472	Lemon
	961	Silver

▪ 18 ▪
After Robert Adam

Difficulty rating: ★★
Design size: 4 x 6¼in (10 x 16cm)
Stitch count: 73 x 113 stitches
Size of canvas needed: 8 x 10¼in (20 x 26cm)

INTRODUCTION

Robert Adam was born in Kirkcaldy, Scotland, in 1728. The son of an architect, he grew up to be an influential architect and interior designer himself. While in his twenties, he spent four years in Italy and on his return he began to develop the 'Adam' style of decoration, very much influenced by what he had seen abroad. He is perhaps best known for his light, elegant interiors, where every detail down to the door handles was designed personally by him. When carpeting his rooms, Robert Adam often collaborated with the carpet manufacturer Thomas Moore of Moorfields, to create knotted pile carpets which reflected the fluid, swirling designs he liked so much.

METHOD

Start in the centre and, using the mustard shade, gradually work outwards until you reach the solid line of this colour. Fill in the main field area with brick red in basketweave stitch. Then complete the border by counting out the width and working a double row of mustard. Fill in with the detail, and finally complete the background in brick red.

After Robert Adam

■	208	Brick red
	693	Mustard

■ 19 ■
After William Morris

Difficulty rating: ★★★
Design size: 9 x 9in (23 x 23cm)
Stitch count: 162 x 162 stitches
Size of canvas needed: 13 x 13in (32.5 x 32.5cm)

INTRODUCTION

Although this is one of the largest designs in the book and uses many colours, it is not impossibly difficult and looks very impressive when completed. Based on the William Morris style, it could suit any room setting from the late 1800s onwards.

William Morris was a talented and creative craftsman of the Victorian era, who became a leading figure in the Socialist movement in later years. He was born in 1834 and, after gaining a degree, he worked in an architect's office. Having financed the

publication of some of his own poems, he soon gave up archi-
tecture for the more creative, if insecure, career of an artist. In
1861 he founded his own company of interior designers, creating
items as diverse as stained-glass windows, furniture and embroi-
dered panels. It was at this stage of his career that he designed
most of his carpets, although he is perhaps best remembered
now for his wallpaper patterns.

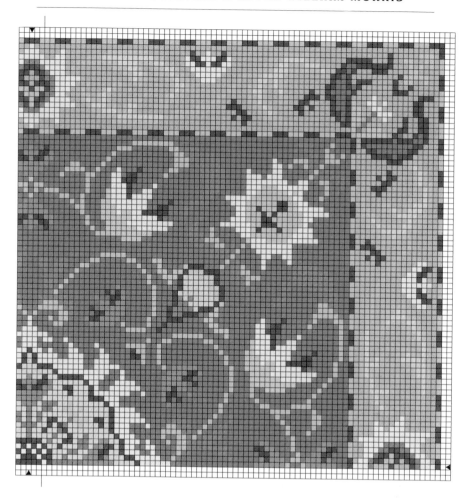

After William Morris

	707	Peach		351	Light grey-green
	862	Dark peach		355	Light moss green
	861	Medium peach		926	Medium blue
	863	Dark coral		924	Dull blue
	352	Grey-green		714	Mulberry

METHOD

Only the top half of the carpet is represented on the chart: the bottom half is exactly the same. When stitching the bottom half, take care not to stitch any rows twice.

Starting with the mulberry shade, work the central medallion area and border, then fill in with the leaves and dark coral flowers. After working the light grey-green background, carefully count the peach medallion border. Next work the grey-green stems and two-tone leaves of the main field. This will make the placing of the various flowers much simpler. Once all the detail of the main area has been completed, work the inner stripey border and, using basketweave stitch, work the dull blue background. As a warning for the faint-hearted, this part alone took me 15 hours!

For the border, start at each corner and work the blue motif, then the peach motif in the centre of each side. This makes it easier to work out the placing of the swirling leaves. Finally work the outer stripey border, and then the border background, using dark peach.

■ 20 ■
Victorian parlour style

Difficulty rating: ★★
Design size: 6 x 6in (15 x 15cm)
Stitch count: 109 x 109 stitches
Size of canvas needed: 10 x 10in (25.5 x 25.5cm)

INTRODUCTION

The Victorians were great lovers of floral designs. They often crammed their rooms with many different patterns which all competed for attention. It was a way of displaying their wealth to the world (or, at the very least, to the neighbours). There was no such thing as a room that was 'too full'. This design uses a rose motif as the basis for a typical Victorian parlour carpet. The busy central design is toned down slightly by the solid pink background. Roses are picked up again for the delicate border pattern.

METHOD

Begin by working the small rose near the centre, then work the larger one. Next work the two lilies in shades of mustard, medium peach and rich brick red. Work the leaves around these flowers, then the tiny pale blue flowers with their mustard-coloured centres. The rosebuds and stems should be worked next, followed by the rest of the leaves and ferns.

To make the background easier to do, first count out the line of the ecru circle before filling it in. Do the same with the baby pink main field area by first working the inner border line of rich brick red, and then 'colouring in' inside it. After that, work the outer border line before stitching the dainty pattern of roses and leaves. Finally fill in the border background with ecru.

For instructions on finishing round carpets, see page 17.

Victorian parlour style

	861	Medium peach		153	Light blue-green
	693	Mustard		741	Pale blue
	882	Ecru		602	Pale purple
	337	Dark sage green		143	Dusty pink
	542	Light green		751	Baby pink
	157	Dark grey-green		505	Rich brick red

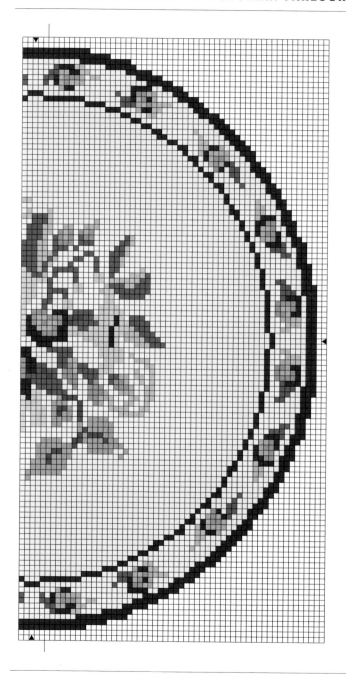

▪ 21 ▪
Chinese style

Difficulty rating: ★★
Design size: 7¾ x 5in (19.5 x 13cm)
Stitch count: 139 x 89 stitches
Size of canvas needed: 11¾ x 9in (30 x 23cm)

INTRODUCTION

The Chinese style of decoration, for everything from porcelain to cabinets, became popular in the seventeenth and early eighteenth centuries, spreading to Britain from Europe. No self-respecting wealthy homeowner of the time would be without his 'Chinese room'. The style was often a very fanciful, and therefore not very accurate, interpretation of Chinese symbols and images. It is very attractive, however, and can be mixed successfully with other styles.

METHOD

Begin by working the centre circle in navy blue, then add the highlights in and around it. Work outwards, finishing off the linear-patterned areas before starting on the curls. Work the inner border line in navy, then fill in the main field in palest peach, using basketweave stitch.

For the border, count out the width and work the single row of dark rust. Then fill in the details, starting with the fleur-de-lys in the centre of each side and working out towards each corner. Finish the design by working the border background in pale rust.

Chinese style

	204	Pale rust		461	Sky blue
	207	Dark rust		747	Navy blue
	704	Palest peach		742	Wedgwood blue

22

Bokhara style

Difficulty rating: ★
Design size: 5 x 4in (13 x 10cm)
Stitch count: 102 x 71 stitches
Size of canvas needed: 9 x 8in (23 x 20cm)

INTRODUCTION

The nomadic Turkoman tribes covered a wide area to the north of Afghanistan and to the east of the Caspian Sea. Bokhara is a village roughly in the centre of this area and in the nineteenth century it was an important trading centre for the nomads. Bartering was the main method of trading, and wool products were considered more valuable than raw wool. Woven carpets, bags and bedding materials were therefore sought-after commodities. The oval motifs which figure prominently on these carpets from Bokhara are known as *guls*. They are thought to be a kind of heraldic symbol, displaying the family lineage of the weaver to those who can decipher the meaning.

METHOD

Start near the centre with one of the ovals and work the burgundy areas for all ten motifs. Using pale stone, surround the centre four squares of each motif. Then fill in the rest of the motifs with chocolate, completing each with an outline of brown-black. Complete the diamond motifs in the same way, starting with pale stone to work the central cross. Count out the brown-black inner border, and fill in the main field with the flesh shade before working the stripes surrounding it. Finally work a double row of flesh and one more of brown-black.

Bokhara style

■	588	Brown-black
■	226	Burgundy
☐	181	Pale stone
■	582	Chocolate
▨	222	Flesh

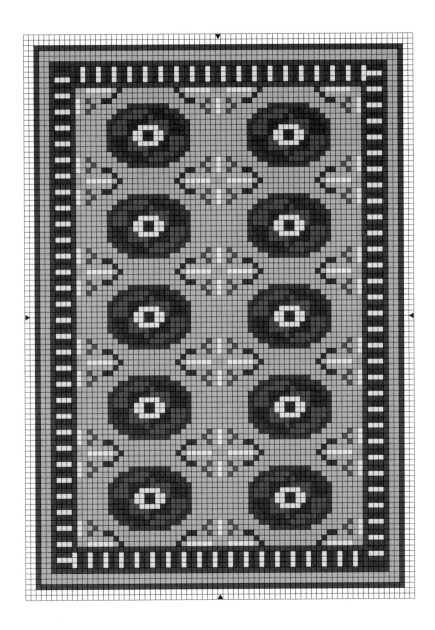

∎ 23 ∎
Turkish style

Difficulty rating: ★★
Design size: 10½ x 6in (26.5 x 15cm)
Stitch count: 189 x 107 stitches
Size of canvas needed: 14½ x 10in (37 x 25.5cm)

INTRODUCTION

There are many styles of Turkish carpet, but they usually feature strong geometric designs. Some fragments of carpets showing traditional designs have been found which date back to AD 200. They have a short, looped pile, made by using what has become known as the hardwearing 'Turkish knot', which experts believe may have been devised to imitate an animal's pelt. This type of fabric would have been used to give protection in a harsh climate. It would not have been created merely for use as an ornate floor covering. By the time of the Victorians, however, who loved everything exotic, these designs were being imported in their thousands to give already overcrowded homes that extra air of opulence.

METHOD

Work the central motif first, building it outwards from the dark sage green cross. Once this motif is finished, the ones either side of it can be completed: the same motif is used, but in a different colourway. Then place the arrowhead motifs around the main field, followed by the dark biscuit brown border and the dull turquoise background, worked in basketweave stitch. Count the width of the inner off-white border and work another single row of dark biscuit brown. Then leave three more rows before working a double row of brown again.

The inner border is simplest to complete if you position the sage green double U-shapes first, followed by the diagonal lines of pale and dark biscuit brown. The rest of the coloured blocks are then easy to position around the border.

For the outer border, work the large and small denim blue triangles, then the green triangles, finishing off with the pale biscuit brown background last of all.

Turkish style

	763	Pale biscuit brown
	767	Dark biscuit brown
	881	Off-white
	332	Sage green
	337	Dark sage green
	522	Dull turquoise
	325	Denim blue

▪ 24 ▪
Persian style

Difficulty rating: ★★★
Design size: 7¾ x 5in (19.5 x 13cm)
Stitch count: 141 x 91 stitches
Size of canvas needed: 11¾ x 9in (30 x 23cm)

INTRODUCTION

This is one of my favourite designs. It is bright and vibrant, and would suit many periods and styles of house. It is a typical Persian design, using several small motifs spread over a bright main field. The shade of red used in this design is characteristic of Persian carpets generally. The designs tend to be very regular in their overall look, and often use only a few colours while still giving a busy appearance.

METHOD

Begin by working the Winchester blue central cross and the square around it. Fill in the cross with the tomato red, then add

the highlights around the cross and the dots of tomato red around the blue square. Next work the bright blue areas in and around this central square, working the pale gold background and zigzag surround last. On the main red field, working out from

the centre, carefully count out the position of the minor motifs, working their main colour first before adding any highlights. Once they have all been completed, it will be easy to work out the position of the Winchester blue inner border line, and the blue and pale gold corner zigzag lines. Fill in the tomato red background in basketweave stitch before moving on to the pale gold corners, where the order of working should be as follows: tomato red first, then Winchester blue, followed by bright blue, with the pale gold background last.

Count out the width of the blue border and work two rows of Winchester blue. Still using this colour, work the narrow central lines of each motif. Working outwards from these lines, complete each motif, then work the corners in the same way, starting with tomato red. Finally fill in the border background using bright blue.

Persian style

■	866	Tomato red
▢	842	Pale gold
▨	564	Bright blue
■	853	Winchester blue

■ 25 ■
Aubusson style

Difficulty rating: ★★★
Design size: 10 x 6in (25.5 x 15cm)
Stitch count: 179 x 109 stitches
Size of canvas needed: 14 x 10in (35.5 x 25.5cm)

INTRODUCTION

This large and subtly shaded design calls for concentration on the floral areas and patience with the plain areas! It is worth persevering, however, as the finished carpet would look lovely in a lady's bedroom or pastel-coloured drawing room.

The design is based on carpets from Aubusson in France. Workshops were established there in 1743 to make carpets for the nobility. Aubusson carpets tend to be large, probably because they were often commissioned by wealthy patrons with large rooms to fill. Although some Aubusson carpets were made to vaguely oriental designs, it is the more delicate Renaissance patterns, such as this one, for which they were better known.

METHOD

Work the dark lilac and pale purple flowers in the centre of the oval medallion first. Stitch the whole of this area before going back over it with palest lemon, picking out the centres. Work the ring of leaves, then the green wavy border with dotted flowers, followed by the wider pale purple oval. Then go back to the centre of the design and fill in with the relevant background shades. Work the swags of flowers and leaves around the oval in the same order as before.

To work out the exact position of the double row of dark lilac for the inner border line, you need to count carefully from one of the outermost leaves on the swag opposite the bowl of flowers, to one of the outermost leaves in the bowl. This will enable you to complete the bowl and flowers, and you can then continue with the dark lilac border that extends from either side. When you reach the corner, you can again use the position of the leaves to count around the corner and give you the correct starting point for the long side border. If you think you might go wrong here, try working only the leaves and border first; if your counting is not accurate, at least you will not have to unpick all those flowers as well! Work the main field background next in pale blue-grey, in basketweave stitch.

For the border, work each corner oval, then count out the pale blue-grey swirls, filling in the background last. Finally complete the design with a row of dark lilac.

Aubusson style

	751	Baby pink
	841	Palest lemon
	153	Light blue-green
	157	Dark grey-green

	886	Pale blue-grey
	104	Dark lilac
	602	Pale purple

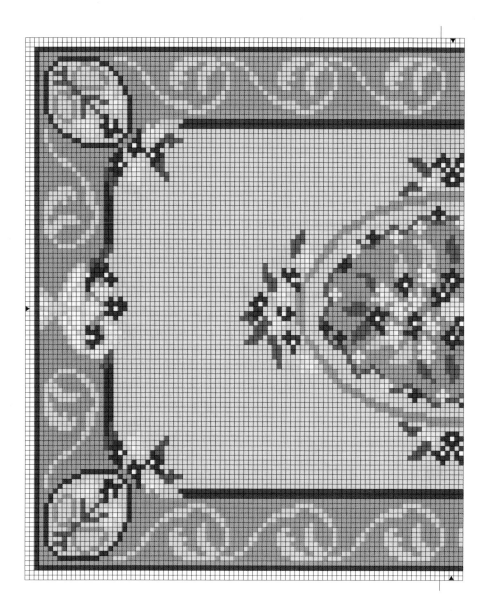

Metric conversion table

Inches to millimetres and centimetres

MM – millimetres **CM – centimetres**

Inches	MM	CM	Inches	CM	Inches	CM
⅛	3	0.3	9	22.9	30	76.2
¼	6	0.6	10	25.4	31	78.7
⅜	10	1.0	11	27.9	32	81.3
½	13	1.3	12	30.5	33	83.8
⅝	16	1.6	13	33.0	34	86.4
¾	19	1.9	14	35.6	35	88.9
⅞	22	2.2	15	38.1	36	91.4
1	25	2.5	16	40.6	37	94.0
1¼	32	3.2	17	43.2	38	96.5
1½	38	3.8	18	45.7	39	99.1
1¾	44	4.4	19	48.3	40	101.6
2	51	5.1	20	50.8	41	104.1
2½	64	6.4	21	53.3	42	106.7
3	76	7.6	22	55.9	43	109.2
3½	89	8.9	23	58.4	44	111.8
4	102	10.2	24	61.0	45	114.3
4½	114	11.4	25	63.5	46	116.8
5	127	12.7	26	66.0	47	119.4
6	152	15.2	27	68.6	48	121.9
7	178	17.8	28	71.1	49	124.5
8	203	20.3	29	73.7	50	127.0

About the author

Janet Granger was born in Hornchurch, Essex. Having worked in the public library for 17 years, she now works in the Learning Resources Centre of a further education college. She has been interested in embroidery since she was 12 years old. Self-taught, she started creating her own designs at the age of 14, and had two exhibitions of her needlework before she was out of her teens.

Designing miniature carpets for dolls' houses has been a growing interest over recent years, and she owns a smart, eight-room Georgian dolls' house. She also runs a small business from home, selling kits for the carpets she designs. Further details and a catalogue can be obtained from Janet at 96 Albert Road, Romford, Essex RM1 2PP.

BOOKS

Woodturning

Adventures in Woodturning	David Springett	Pleasure & Profit from Woodturning	Reg Sher
Bert Marsh: Woodturner	Bert Marsh	Practical Tips for Turners & Carvers	GMC Publicat
Bill Jones' Notes from the Turning Shop	Bill Jones	Practical Tips for Woodturners	GMC Publicat
Carving on Turning	Chris Pye	Spindle Turning	GMC Publicat
Colouring Techniques for Woodturners	Jan Sanders	Turning Miniatures in Wood	John Sainsk
Decorative Techniques for Woodturners	Hilary Bowen	Turning Wooden Toys	Terry Lawre
Faceplate Turning: Features, Projects, Practice	GMC Publications	Useful Woodturning Projects	GMC Publicat
Green Woodwork	Mike Abbott	Woodturning: A Foundation Course	Keith Rov
Illustrated Woodturning Techniques	John Hunnex	Woodturning Jewellery	Hilary Bo
Keith Rowley's Woodturning Projects	Keith Rowley	Woodturning Masterclass	Tony B
Make Money from Woodturning	Ann & Bob Phillips	Woodturning: A Source Book of Shapes	John Hui
Multi-Centre Woodturning	Ray Hopper	Woodturning Techniques	GMC Publicat
		Woodturning Wizardry	David Sprin

Woodcarving

The Art of the Woodcarver	GMC Publications	Wildfowl Carving Volume 1	Jim Pea
Carving Birds & Beasts	GMC Publications	Wildfowl Carving Volume 2	Jim Pea
Carving Realistic Birds	David Tippey	Woodcarving: A Complete Course	Ron Butterf
Carving on Turning	Chris Pye	Woodcarving for Beginners: Projects, Techniques & Tools	
Decorative Woodcarving	Jeremy Williams		GMC Publicati
Practical Tips for Turners & Carvers	GMC Publications	Woodcarving Tools, Materials & Equipment	Chris

Plans, Projects, Tools & the Workshop

40 More Woodworking Plans & Projects	GMC Publications	Sharpening: The Complete Guide	Jim Kingsh
Electric Woodwork: Power Tool Woodworking	Jeremy Broun	Sharpening Pocket Reference Book	Jim Kingsh
The Incredible Router	Jeremy Broun	Woodworking Plans & Projects	GMC Publicatic
Making & Modifying Woodworking Tools	Jim Kingshott	The Workshop	Jim Kingsh

Toys & Miniatures

Designing & Making Wooden Toys	Terry Kelly	Making Wooden Toys & Games	Jeff & Jennie Loac
Heraldic Miniature Knights	Peter Greenhill	Miniature Needlepoint Carpets	Janet Grans
Making Board, Peg & Dice Games	Jeff & Jennie Loader	Restoring Rocking Horses	Clive Green & Anthony D
Making Little Boxes from Wood	John Bennett	Turning Miniatures in Wood	John Sainsbu
Making Unusual Miniatures	Graham Spalding	Turning Wooden Toys	Terry Lawren

Creative Crafts

The Complete Pyrography	Stephen Poole	Creating Knitwear Designs	Pat Ashforth & Steve Plumm
Cross Stitch on Colour	Sheena Rogers	Making Knitwear Fit	Pat Ashforth & Steve Plumm
Embroidery Tips & Hints	Harold Hayes	Miniature Needlepoint Carpets	Janet Grans
		Tatting Collage: Adventurous Ideas for Tatters	Lindsay Roge

UPHOLSTERY AND FURNITURE

Care & Repair	GMC Publications
Complete Woodfinishing	Ian Hosker
Furniture Projects	Rod Wales
Furniture Restoration (Practical Crafts)	Kevin Jan Bonner
Furniture Restoration & Repair for Beginners	Kevin Jan Bonner
Green Woodwork	Mike Abbott
Making Fine Furniture	Tom Darby
Making Shaker Furniture	Barry Jackson
Seat Weaving (Practical Crafts)	Ricky Holdstock
Upholsterer's Pocket Reference Book	David James
Upholstery: A Complete Course	David James
Upholstery: Techniques & Projects	David James
Woodfinishing Handbook (Practical Crafts)	Ian Hosker

DOLLS' HOUSES & DOLLS' HOUSE FURNITURE

Architecture for Dolls' Houses	Joyce Percival
The Complete Dolls' House Book	Jean Nisbett
Easy-to-Make Dolls' House Accessories	Andrea Barham
Make Your Own Dolls' House Furniture	Maurice Harper
Making Dolls' House Furniture	Patricia King
Making Georgian Dolls' Houses	Derek Rowbottom
Making Period Dolls' House Accessories	Andrea Barham
Making Period Dolls' House Furniture	Derek & Sheila Rowbottom
Making Tudor Dolls' Houses	Derek Rowbottom
Making Victorian Dolls' House Furniture	Patricia King
Miniature Needlepoint Carpets	Janet Granger
The Secrets of the Dolls' House Makers	Jean Nisbett

OTHER BOOKS

Guide to Marketing	GMC Publications
Woodworkers' Career & Educational Source Book	GMC Publications

VIDEOS

Carving a Figure: The Female Form	Ray Gonzalez
The Traditional Upholstery Workshop Part 1: Drop-in & Pinstuffed Seats	David James
The Traditional Upholstery Workshop Part 2: Stuffover Upholstery	David James
Hollow Turning	John Jordan
Bowl Turning	John Jordan
Sharpening Turning & Carving Tools	Jim Kingshott
Sharpening the Professional Way	Jim Kingshott
Elliptical Turning	David Springett
Woodturning Wizardry	David Springett
Turning Between Centres: The Basics	Dennis White
Turning Bowls	Dennis White
Boxes, Goblets & Screw Threads	Dennis White
Novelties & Projects	Dennis White
Classic Profiles	Dennis White
Twists & Advanced Turning	Dennis White

MAGAZINES

WOODTURNING ● WOODCARVING ● BUSINESSMATTERS

The above represents a full list of all titles currently published or scheduled to be published. All are available direct from the Publishers or through bookshops, newsagents and specialist retailers. To place an order, or to obtain a complete catalogue, contact:

GMC Publications, 166 High Street, Lewes, East Sussex BN7 1XU United Kingdom
Tel: 01273 488005 Fax: 01273 478606

Orders by credit card are accepted